Harry M. Thomas

The Price of Ambition

Harry M. Thomas

1

Harry M. Thomas

Harry M. Thomas

Table of Contents

Harry M. Thomas

Conclusion

Introduction

In a world where success is everything, where the line between ambition and obsession is blurred, one man's journey stands out above all others. His name is Johnathon Richards, and his story is one of the most riveting tales of wealth, power, and the high cost of achieving them.

As a young man, Johnathon was filled with a burning desire to succeed. He had a clear vision of his future, one where he would rise to the top of the business world and become a titan of industry. And with his razor-sharp mind and relentless work ethic, he was well on his way to achieving his dreams.

But as Johnathon's wealth and power grew, so too did his ambition. He became consumed by the pursuit of success, driven to do whatever it takes to climb higher and higher. His once unshakeable moral compass began to waver, and he found himself making deals that left a trail of destruction in his wake.

As Johnathon navigated the cutthroat world of business, he became increasingly isolated from those around him. His relationships with his family and friends suffered, and he found himself increasingly alone with his thoughts and ambitions. And yet, even as his success seemed assured, he couldn't shake the feeling that something was missing.

Through all the trials and tribulations of his journey, Johnathon must grapple with some of the most profound questions of human existence. What is the price of success? Is there a limit to what one should do to achieve their dreams? And perhaps most importantly, what is the true meaning of happiness?

As you embark on this unforgettable journey with Johnathon, prepare to be swept away by a story that will challenge your beliefs, tug at your heartstrings, and leave you breathless until the very end. For in the world of "Fortune's Price", anything is possible, and the price of success is always just a little bit higher than you think.

Chapter one

The Beginning

Johnathon had always dreamed of making it big. He grew up in a small town, surrounded by poverty and struggle, but he knew he was destined for something greater. He was driven, ambitious, and willing to do whatever it took to achieve success.

At a young age, Johnathon discovered his talent for entrepreneurship. He started small, selling candy and toys to his classmates, but soon he was running a thriving business out of his garage.

As he grew older, Johnathon's ambitions grew with him. He saw opportunities everywhere he looked, and he was determined to seize them all. He worked long hours, sacrificed his social life, and poured every ounce of energy into building his empire.

It wasn't easy. There were setbacks, failures, and disappointments along the way. But Johnathon refused to let these obstacles stop him. He learned from his mistakes, adapted to new challenges, and kept pushing forward.

And it paid off. Soon, Johnathon was the talk of the town. His business had expanded beyond the borders of his small community, and he was making a name for himself in the wider world of entrepreneurship.

But Johnathon knew that this was just the beginning. He wanted more. He wanted to be the biggest, the best, the most successful. And he was willing to do whatever it took to get there.

So he kept grinding. He invested in new ventures, hired talented employees, and took calculated risks. And with each passing day, his empire grew stronger and more impressive.

But as Johnathon would soon discover, success always comes with a price. And he would have to pay dearly for his ambitions.

As Johnathon's wealth and influence grew, so did his sense of entitlement. He became obsessed with power and control, and he was willing to do whatever it took to maintain his position at the top.

He began to view his competitors as enemies to be crushed, rather than fellow entrepreneurs to be respected. He engaged in unethical business practices, cut corners, and disregarded the needs of his employees and customers.

Despite his success, Johnathon felt

unfulfilled. He realized that his relentless pursuit of wealth and power had come at a cost. He had sacrificed his relationships, his values, and his sense of purpose.

And so, Johnathon found himself at a crossroads. He could continue down the path of ruthless ambition, or he could choose a different way.

It was a difficult decision, but in the end, Johnathon realized that he wanted more from life than just wealth and power. He wanted to make a positive impact on the world, to leave a legacy that went beyond material success.

And so, he began to shift his priorities. He invested in ethical business practices, prioritized the well-being of his employees and customers, and supported charitable causes that aligned with his values.

It was a slow process, and there were many obstacles along the way. But Johnathon was determined to change course, to use his resources for good, and to leave a positive impact on the world.

And so, his journey continued, but this time, with a different purpose in mind. He knew that the road ahead would be challenging, but he was ready to face whatever obstacles lay in his path. He was ready to be a force for good in the world, to use his wealth and influence to make a positive difference, and to leave a legacy that would be remembered long after he was gone.

As Johnathon continued on his new path, he faced many challenges and setbacks. He had to navigate the complexities of ethical business practices, learn how to balance his ambition with compassion, and overcome the mistrust that his past actions had created.

But he refused to give up. He was determined to prove that success and morality were not mutually exclusive, and that it was possible to use one's resources for good without sacrificing financial gain.

Slowly but surely, Johnathon began to rebuild his reputation. He gained the trust and respect of his employees and customers, and he became known as a leader who prioritized ethics and integrity over profits and power.

And as his influence grew, Johnathon began to use his platform to advocate for social justice and equality. He supported causes that aligned with his values, such as environmental sustainability, education, and human rights.

It wasn't an easy journey, but Johnathon knew that it was worth it. He had found a sense of purpose that went beyond material success, and he was using his wealth and influence to make a positive difference in the world.

As he reflected on his journey, Johnathon realized that the beginning of his story was just the tip of the iceberg. There was so much more to come, so many more challenges to overcome, and so many more opportunities to create a better world.

And so, he continued on his path, driven by a sense of purpose and a desire to leave a positive legacy. For Johnathon, the beginning was just the start of an incredible journey, and he was excited to see where it would lead.

Chapter Two

The Early Years

Johnathon was born into a humble family, in a small town in the Midwest. His parents worked long hours to make ends meet, and Johnathon learned the value of hard work and perseverance at a young age.

From a young age, Johnathon was always fascinated by business. He would watch in awe as his father managed the family's small grocery store, interacting with customers, managing inventory, and ensuring that the business ran smoothly.

It wasn't long before Johnathon began to develop his own entrepreneurial spirit. He would set up lemonade stands in front of the grocery store, selling cold drinks to passersby. He would collect discarded cans and bottles, and sell them to recycling centers for a small profit. And he would even offer to mow lawns for his neighbors, earning a few extra dollars to put towards his savings.

Despite his young age, Johnathon was already showing signs of the ambition and drive that would propel him to success later in life.

As he grew older, Johnathon's interest in business only intensified. He spent hours reading books on entrepreneurship, studying the strategies of successful businessmen, and dreaming of starting his own business someday.

And when he graduated from high school, he knew that he wanted to pursue a career in business. He enrolled in a local community college, studying business administration and marketing, and working part-time jobs to pay for his tuition.

It wasn't easy, but Johnathon was determined to succeed. He spent countless hours studying and working, determined to build the skills and knowledge that he needed to achieve his goals.

And it wasn't long before Johnathon's hard work began to pay off. He landed an internship at a local marketing firm, where he impressed his bosses with his creativity and innovation. And when he graduated from college, he was offered a full-time job at the firm.

For Johnathon, it was a dream come true. He was finally working in the field that he was passionate about, surrounded by like-minded professionals who shared his ambition and drive.

And as he worked his way up the corporate ladder, Johnathon began to realize that he had the potential to achieve even greater things. He knew that he was destined for success, and he was determined to make his mark on the world of business.

But little did he know, his journey was only just beginning.

As Johnathon continued to climb the corporate ladder, he faced his fair share of challenges and setbacks. He worked long hours, sacrificed his personal life, and faced fierce competition from his colleagues.

But Johnathon was undeterred. He was determined to prove himself, and he worked tirelessly to hone his skills and knowledge, taking on new projects and responsibilities with enthusiasm and dedication.

And his hard work paid off. Within a few years, Johnathon had been promoted to a high-level management position, with a six-figure salary and a team of employees reporting to him.

For Johnathon, it was a dream come true. He was finally earning the kind of money that he had always dreamed of, and he was in a position of power and influence that gave him the ability to make a real impact.

But as he settled into his new role, Johnathon began to notice something troubling. Many of the decisions that he and his colleagues were making seemed to prioritize profits over ethics, and he began to feel uneasy about the way that the company was operating.

He watched as his colleagues cut corners and made decisions that were detrimental to the environment and the community, all in the pursuit of financial gain. And he began to wonder whether this was really the kind of business that he wanted to be a part of.

As Johnathon struggled with these doubts and uncertainties, he found himself at a crossroads. He could either continue on his current path, chasing money and power at any cost, or he could take a different approach and prioritize ethics and morality in his work.

It wasn't an easy decision, but ultimately Johnathon chose the latter. He realized that he couldn't continue to compromise his values in the pursuit of wealth, and that he needed to find a way to use his skills and resources for good.

And so, he set out on a new path, one that would take him on a journey of self-discovery, growth, and ultimately, success on his own terms.

Little did Johnathon know, his decision would change the course of his life forever, leading him on a journey that would take him places he had never imagined, and ultimately, to a place of fulfillment and purpose beyond his wildest dreams.

As Johnathon began to explore his options for a more ethical and sustainable career path, he discovered the world of impact investing. He learned about investors who sought to support companies that were making a positive impact on society and the environment, and he was immediately drawn to the idea.

He spent months researching different

companies and industries, seeking out those that aligned with his values and beliefs. And eventually, he found a company that he believed in, one that was dedicated to creating sustainable products and services, and making a positive impact on the world.

Without hesitation, Johnathon resigned from his high-paying job and joined the company, eager to use his skills and expertise to make a real difference. And although he had to adjust to a lower salary and a different pace of life, he felt a sense of purpose and fulfillment that he had never experienced before.

In his new role, Johnathon was able to use his business acumen to help the company grow and succeed, while also staying true to his values and beliefs. He worked alongside a team of like-minded individuals who were passionate about creating positive change, and together, they achieved remarkable success.

As the years passed, Johnathon rose through the ranks of the company, eventually becoming its CEO. And under his leadership, the company grew exponentially, becoming a leader in the world of sustainable business.

For Johnathon, it was the ultimate success story. He had found a way to use his skills and resources to create positive change in the world, while also achieving financial stability and personal fulfillment.

And as he looked back on his journey, he realized that it had all started with his humble beginnings, growing up in a small town in the Midwest, with a dream of making it in the world of business.

Little did he know, his journey was only just beginning, and the best was yet to come.

Chapter Three

The Price of Success

Johnathon had found success in his new role at the sustainable business, but he soon realized that it came with a price. He was working longer hours than ever before, often sacrificing his personal life and time with his family to meet the demands of his job.

Despite the sacrifices, Johnathon was driven by his passion and sense of purpose. He believed that he was making a difference in the world, and that his work was helping to create a better future for generations to come.

But as the months passed, Johnathon began to feel the toll that his demanding job was taking on his health and well-being. He was constantly stressed and exhausted, struggling to find balance in his life.

He began to question whether it was all worth it, whether the price of success was too high. He had achieved his dreams of financial stability and personal fulfillment, but at what cost?

Johnathon knew that he needed to find a way to prioritize his health and well-being, without sacrificing the work that he was passionate about. He began to explore different strategies for managing stress and achieving balance in his life.

He started to prioritize exercise and healthy eating, making time for daily workouts and cooking healthy meals at home. He also began to set boundaries in his work life, learning to say no to projects and tasks that didn't align with his priorities and values.

Slowly but surely, Johnathon began to find a sense of balance in his life. He was still dedicated to his work, but he was also making time for the things that mattered most to him, like spending time with his family and pursuing his hobbies and interests.

And as he found this balance, Johnathon realized that he was even more effective in his work. He had more energy and focus, and was able to approach his job with renewed passion and dedication.

In the end, Johnathon learned that success didn't have to come at the cost of his health and well-being. With the right strategies and priorities, he was able to achieve both, creating a fulfilling and sustainable life that he was proud of.

As Johnathon continued to prioritize

his health and well-being, he also began to think more deeply about the nature of success. He realized that success wasn't just about financial wealth or professional achievements, but also about living a life that was meaningful and fulfilling.

He started to question the traditional definitions of success that he had grown up with, and began to explore new ideas and perspectives. He read books on mindfulness and spirituality, attended workshops on personal growth and development, and sought out new experiences that challenged his beliefs and expanded his horizons.

Through these experiences, Johnathon began to see success in a whole new light. He realized that it wasn't just about achieving external goals or accumulating wealth, but about living a life that was aligned with his values and beliefs, and that brought him a sense of purpose and fulfillment.

With this new perspective, Johnathon began to approach his work in a different way. He was still committed to creating positive change and making a difference in the world, but he also recognized the importance of taking care of himself and finding joy and fulfillment in his personal life.

And as he continued on this journey, Johnathon discovered that success was not a destination, but a lifelong journey. It was about finding balance and meaning in all aspects of his life, and continually striving to grow and evolve as a person.

In the end, Johnathon realized that the price of success was not just the sacrifices he had made along the way, but also the willingness to challenge his own beliefs and perceptions, and to embrace a new and more fulfilling definition of success. And he knew that this journey was far from over, but he was excited to continue on this path, wherever it may lead him.

As Johnathon reflected on his journey, he couldn't help but feel grateful for the people who had supported him along the way. From his family and friends to his mentors and colleagues, he had been surrounded by a community of people who believed in him and his vision.

He realized that his success was not just the result of his own hard work and determination, but also the result of the support and guidance of others. And he knew that it was important to pay it forward, and to help others achieve their own dreams and goals.

With this in mind, Johnathon began to look for ways to give back to his community. He volunteered at local non-profits and charities, mentoring young professionals and aspiring entrepreneurs, and sharing his knowledge and expertise with others.

Through his volunteer work, Johnathon discovered a new sense of purpose and fulfillment, and realized that giving back was just as important as achieving his own personal goals.

As he continued on his journey, Johnathon knew that there would be challenges and setbacks along the way. But he also knew that he had the tools and support he needed to overcome them, and that he would always be guided by his passion and sense of purpose.

And he was excited to see where this

journey would take him next, knowing that he had the power to create a life that was both successful and fulfilling, in every sense of the word.

As Johnathon approached the end of his third chapter, he felt a deep sense of gratitude and optimism. He knew that he had come a long way, but he also recognized that there was still much to learn and experience on his journey towards success and fulfillment.

He was excited to continue to explore new ideas and perspectives, to challenge his own beliefs and perceptions, and to give back to his community in meaningful ways.

And he knew that with the right mindset, support, and hard work, anything was possible. He was confident that he could create a life that was both successful and fulfilling, and he was eager to see what the future held.

As he closed the chapter on this phase of his journey, Johnathon felt a renewed sense of energy and purpose, ready to take on whatever challenges and opportunities lay ahead. He knew that the road ahead would be long and winding, but he was determined to embrace the journey, every step of the way.

Chapter Four

Taking Risks and Embracing Failure

As Johnathon continued on his journey towards success and fulfillment, he realized that taking risks was an essential part of the process. He knew that in order to achieve his goals, he needed to be willing to step outside of his comfort zone and try new things, even if it meant facing the possibility of failure.

At first, the idea of failure was daunting to Johnathon. Like many people, he had been raised to believe that failure was something to be avoided at all costs, and that success was only attainable through flawless execution and careful planning.

But as he gained more experience and wisdom, Johnathon began to see failure in a different light. He realized that failure was not a sign of weakness or incompetence, but rather a necessary part of growth and learning.

Through his own failures and setbacks, Johnathon had learned some of his most valuable lessons, and had gained the resilience and perseverance needed to overcome future challenges.

With this newfound perspective, Johnathon began to take more risks in his personal and professional life. He launched new projects and pursued new opportunities, even if they seemed daunting or uncertain.

And while he faced his fair share of failures and setbacks along the way, he also experienced great success and fulfillment, and learned that taking risks was an essential part of achieving his goals.

Through it all, Johnathon remained committed to his core values and purpose, never losing sight of what was truly important to him. And he knew that even in the face of failure, he had the resilience and determination needed to bounce back and continue on his journey towards success and fulfillment.

As Johnathon embraced failure as a necessary part of his journey, he also learned to approach it in a more productive and positive way. Rather than dwelling on his mistakes or beating himself up for his shortcomings, he chose to view failure as an opportunity for growth and learning.

He asked himself, "What can I learn from this experience? How can I use this setback to make me stronger and more resilient? How can I approach this situation differently in the future?"

By reframing failure in this way, Johnathon was able to stay motivated and focused, even in the face of setbacks and obstacles. He was able to stay committed to his goals and values, and to continue moving forward towards his vision for success and fulfillment.

Of course, taking risks and embracing failure was not always easy. There were times when Johnathon felt uncertain or overwhelmed, and times when he faced harsh criticism or rejection.

But he never lost sight of his purpose or his passion, and he remained committed to his journey, even when the road ahead seemed difficult or uncertain.

Through it all, Johnathon realized that success and fulfillment were not just about achieving a specific goal or reaching a certain level of wealth or status. Rather, they were about embracing the journey itself, and living a life that was true to his values and purpose.

As Johnathon closed the chapter on his journey of taking risks and embracing failure, he felt a deep sense of gratitude and optimism. He knew that the road ahead would continue to be challenging, but he also knew that he had the resilience and determination needed to overcome any obstacle that came his way.

And he was excited to see where his

journey would take him next, eager to continue exploring new ideas and perspectives, and to embrace whatever challenges and opportunities lay ahead.

As Johnathon reflected on his journey so far, he realized that taking risks and embracing failure had been key to his growth and success. He had learned to approach challenges with a positive and productive mindset, and to use setbacks as opportunities for learning and growth.

Through it all, he had remained committed to his core values and purpose, and had never lost sight of his vision for success and fulfillment.

And as he looked ahead to the next chapter of his journey, Johnathon knew that he had the skills, mindset, and determination needed to continue on the path towards his goals and dreams.

He knew that there would be more challenges and setbacks along the way, but he was ready to face them head-on, armed with the knowledge and experience he had gained thus far.

With a sense of optimism and excitement, Johnathon closed the chapter on taking risks and embracing failure, eager to see what the next chapter of his journey would hold.

Chapter 5

Building a Strong Support System

As Johnathon continued on his journey towards success and fulfillment, he realized that he couldn't do it alone. He needed a strong support system to help him along the way.

But what did a strong support system look like? For Johnathon, it meant having people in his life who believed in him, encouraged him, and held him accountable. It meant surrounding himself with individuals who shared his values and aspirations, and who could offer guidance and support when he needed it most.

So, he set out to build his support

system. He reached out to mentors and coaches who could offer him guidance and advice. He sought out like-minded individuals who shared his passion for personal growth and development. And he worked to strengthen his existing relationships with friends and family, cultivating deeper connections and communication.

As he built his support system, Johnathon realized that it wasn't just about having people in his life who could offer him help and advice. It was also about being there for others, and giving back to those who had supported him along the way.

He began to look for opportunities to be of service, volunteering his time and resources to causes and organizations he cared about. He made a point of showing up for his friends and family, offering a listening ear and a helping hand whenever they needed it.

Through it all, Johnathon learned that building a strong support system was about more than just having people in his life who could offer him help and advice. It was about cultivating meaningful connections and relationships, and giving back to the community around him.

As he continued on his journey, Johnathon knew that his support system would be there for him through both the highs and lows. And he was grateful for the people in his life who had helped him along the way, and who would continue to be there for him in the years to come.

As Johnathon strengthened his support system, he noticed a shift in his mindset and approach to life. He no longer felt like he was navigating his journey alone. Instead, he felt supported and encouraged by the people in his life who believed in him and his vision for success and fulfillment.

With this newfound support and encouragement, Johnathon felt empowered to take bigger risks and pursue his goals with even greater passion and determination. He knew that he had a team of people in his corner, ready to help him overcome any obstacles that he might encounter along the way.

And as he continued to build his support system, Johnathon noticed that he was also developing a greater sense of gratitude and appreciation for the people in his life. He recognized the incredible impact that his support system had on his life, and he was committed to showing his appreciation and giving back in any way that he could.

Through his journey of building a strong support system, Johnathon learned that success and fulfillment were not achieved alone. They were the result of hard work, determination, and the support and encouragement of those around us.

As he closed the chapter on building a strong support system, Johnathon was grateful for the people in his life who had helped him along the way, and excited for the next chapter of his journey. He knew that with his support system by his side, he could achieve anything he set his mind to.

As Johnathon reflected on his journey so far, he realized that building a strong support system was just the beginning. There was still much work to be done, and he knew that he couldn't do it alone. But with the support and encouragement of his team, he was ready to take on whatever challenges lay ahead.

With renewed energy and determination, Johnathon set his sights on his next goal. He was ready to push himself further than ever before, and he was confident that he had the support system in place to help him succeed.

As he looked ahead to the future, Johnathon knew that his journey would not always be easy. There would be obstacles and setbacks, but he was prepared to face them head-on. With his support system by his side, he knew that he could overcome any challenge and achieve his dreams.

With a deep sense of gratitude and appreciation for the people in his life, Johnathon closed the chapter on building a strong support system and prepared to embark on the next phase of his journey. He knew that whatever lay ahead, he was ready to face it with courage, determination, and the unwavering support of his team.

As Johnathon continued on his journey towards success and fulfillment, he realized that he needed to focus on personal growth and development. He knew that in order to achieve his goals, he needed to constantly be learning and improving himself.

With this in mind, Johnathon set out to expand his knowledge and skills in a variety of areas. He read books on leadership, entrepreneurship, and personal development, attended workshops and seminars, and even took classes at a local community college.

As he delved deeper into his studies, Johnathon began to see the world in a new light. He realized that there was so much he didn't know, and he became eager to learn as much as he could. He was fascinated by the ways in which knowledge and skills could be applied to create positive change in the world.

As he grew and developed personally, Johnathon also saw a positive impact on his professional life. He was able to bring new ideas and perspectives to his work, and he was more confident in his ability to take on new challenges and opportunities.

But Johnathon knew that personal growth and development were not just about achieving success in his career. It was also about becoming a better person and contributing to the world in a positive way. He made a commitment to use his newfound knowledge and skills to help others and make a difference in his community.

As he closed the chapter on personal growth and development, Johnathon was excited to see where his journey would take him next. He knew that he still had much to learn and improve upon, but he was confident that with hard work and dedication, he could achieve anything he set his mind to.

Chapter six

Taking Action

With his support system in place and his personal growth underway, Johnathon was ready to take action towards achieving his goals. He had spent enough time planning and preparing, and now it was time to put his ideas into motion.

Johnathon began by setting clear and specific goals for himself. He broke them down into smaller, more manageable tasks that he could work on every day. He also established deadlines for himself, which helped him stay accountable and motivated.

As he started working towards his goals, Johnathon encountered some challenges along the way. There were times when he felt discouraged and doubted his abilities. But he was determined to push through and stay focused on his end goal.

One thing that helped Johnathon stay on track was his willingness to ask for help when he needed it. He reached out to his support system for advice and encouragement, and they were always there to lift him up when he was feeling down.

Another key factor in Johnathon's success was his willingness to take risks. He knew that in order to achieve his goals, he would need to step outside of his comfort zone and try new things. He wasn't afraid to fail, and he saw each setback as an opportunity to learn and grow.

As he worked towards his goals, Johnathon began to see progress. He was accomplishing things that he never thought possible, and he felt a sense of pride and accomplishment in his work. He was making a difference in his community and contributing to the world in a positive way.

As he closed the chapter on taking action, Johnathon knew that there was still much work to be done. But he was confident in his abilities and committed to staying focused on his goals. He was ready to face whatever challenges lay ahead, knowing that with hard work and determination, he could achieve anything he set his mind to.

With each passing day, Johnathon grew more and more confident in his abilities. He had developed a strong work ethic and a deep sense of determination, and he was willing to do whatever it took to achieve his goals.

One of the things that had helped Johnathon stay motivated was his ability to track his progress. He kept a journal where he documented his successes and failures, and he regularly reviewed his goals to ensure that he was on the right track.

In addition to tracking his progress, Johnathon also made a point to celebrate his successes. He acknowledged the hard work and dedication that had gone into achieving his goals, and he allowed himself to feel proud of his accomplishments.

As he continued on his journey, Johnathon also began to see the impact that his actions were having on others. He received messages of support and encouragement from people in his community, and he knew that he was making a difference in the world.

But despite all of his successes, Johnathon remained humble and grounded. He knew that there was still much work to be done, and he was committed to continuing on his path of personal growth and development.

As he closed the chapter on his journey of taking action, Johnathon knew that he had come a long way. He had faced challenges and overcome obstacles, and he had grown in ways that he never thought possible. But he also knew that there was still much more to be accomplished, and he was excited to see where his journey would take him next.

With a renewed sense of purpose and determination, Johnathon embarked on the next phase of his journey. He knew that in order to continue growing and achieving his goals, he needed to keep pushing himself out of his comfort zone and taking on new challenges.

One of the biggest challenges that Johnathon faced was finding a way to balance his newfound success with his personal life. As he became more successful, he found himself struggling to find time for his friends and family, and he often felt overwhelmed by the demands of his work.

But Johnathon was determined to find a way to balance his personal and professional life. He began to prioritize his time more effectively, setting aside specific times for work and for spending time with loved ones. He also made a point to take care of himself, making sure to get enough sleep, eat a healthy diet, and exercise regularly.

As he continued on his journey, Johnathon also began to seek out new opportunities for personal and professional growth. He attended workshops and seminars, networked with other successful individuals, and pursued new hobbies and interests.

Through it all, Johnathon remained focused on his long-term goals and the impact that he wanted to have on the world. He knew that he had been given a gift, and he was determined to use it to make a difference in the lives of others.

As he approached the end of this chapter of his journey, Johnathon felt a sense of pride and accomplishment. He had faced numerous challenges and overcome them all, and he had grown in ways that he never thought possible. But he also knew that there was still much more work to be done, and he was excited to see where his journey would take him next.

With a sense of gratitude for how far he had come, Johnathon reflected on the lessons he had learned on his journey. He realized that success wasn't just about achieving his goals, but also about the person he became in the process.

He had learned the importance of perseverance, hard work, and discipline. He had learned that setbacks and failures were simply opportunities to learn and grow. And he had learned that the most fulfilling way to live was to use his talents and abilities to make a positive impact on the world.

As he closed the chapter on this phase of his journey, Johnathon felt a renewed sense of purpose and determination. He knew that there were still many challenges ahead, but he was confident in his ability to face them head-on.

With a deep sense of gratitude for the journey that had brought him to this point, Johnathon took a deep breath and prepared to embark on the next phase of his journey, eager to see where it would take him next.

Chapter Seven

Building a Legacy

As Johnathon continued to grow his wealth, he began to think more about the legacy he wanted to leave behind. He knew that money alone would not be enough to create a lasting impact on the world. He needed to use his resources and influence to make a positive difference in people's lives.

Johnathon began to research different ways he could give back to his community. He attended philanthropy events, met with charity organizations, and learned about the different ways he could contribute to causes he cared about.

After much thought and consideration, Johnathon decided to start his own charitable foundation. He called it the

"Johnson Legacy Foundation," and its mission was to help underprivileged children in his local community.

Johnathon invested a significant portion of his wealth into the foundation, and he worked tirelessly to build relationships with local schools and community centers. He wanted to make sure that the foundation's resources were being used to maximum effect.

Over time, the Johnson Legacy Foundation became a respected and influential organization in the community. Its programs helped countless children get access to education, health care, and other resources that they otherwise would not have had.

But Johnathon's legacy went beyond just his charitable work. He was also known for being a mentor to young entrepreneurs, helping them navigate the ups and downs of building a successful business. He believed that it was his responsibility to use his own success to help others achieve their own dreams.

As Johnathon looked back on his life, he felt proud of the legacy he had built. He knew that his wealth had given him the opportunity to make a real difference in the world, and he was grateful for that.

But he also knew that his legacy was not yet complete. There were still so many ways he could use his resources and influence to make an even greater impact on the world. And he was excited to see what the future held, knowing that there was still so much he could accomplish.

One of the ways Johnathon planned to further his impact was by expanding the reach of his foundation. He began to explore ways to partner with other organizations and donors to support larger-scale initiatives.

Through his network of contacts, Johnathon was able to connect with other philanthropists who shared his vision for creating positive change in the world. They worked together to fund projects that tackled issues such as poverty, healthcare access, and education on a global scale.

As his philanthropic work continued to grow, Johnathon became a sought-after speaker at conferences and events. He shared his experiences and insights with other business leaders, encouraging them to use their own success to create positive change.

But Johnathon's commitment to his legacy went beyond just his philanthropic work. He also wanted to ensure that his business would continue to thrive long after he was gone. He began grooming his son to take over the family business, teaching him the skills and values that had led to his own success.

Johnathon knew that building a legacy wasn't just about what he did while he was alive. It was also about the impact he would have long after he was gone. By investing in his family and his community, Johnathon was creating a lasting impact that would be felt for generations to come.

As Johnathon reflected on his journey, he realized that his success was not just due to his own hard work and dedication. He had been blessed with opportunities and support along the way, and he was grateful for all of the people who had helped him achieve his goals.

With that in mind, Johnathon redoubled his commitment to giving back. He continued to invest in his foundation and his community, and he encouraged others to do the same.

As Johnathon entered the later years of his life, he knew that his legacy was secure. He had built a successful business, created a charitable foundation that helped countless children, and inspired others to use their own success for the greater good.

And while he may not have been able to change the world on his own, Johnathon knew that every small act of kindness and generosity added up to create a brighter future for all.

As Johnathon's life drew to a close, he

felt a sense of peace and fulfillment knowing that he had lived a life of purpose and meaning. He had used his success to make a difference in the world, and he had inspired others to do the same.

In his final days, Johnathon gathered his family and closest friends around him. He shared stories of his journey, and reminded them of the importance of using their own success to give back to others.

As he took his last breath, Johnathon knew that his legacy would live on through his family, his foundation, and all of the lives he had touched along the way.

And while his time on earth may have been limited, Johnathon's impact would continue to ripple through the world for generations to come.

Harry M. Thomas

Chapter Eight

A New Beginning

As the sun began to rise on a new day, Johnathon Richards sat at his desk with a sense of unease. He had recently made the decision to leave his high-paying job at a large corporation and strike out on his own, but now that the moment had finally arrived, he couldn't help but feel a sense of fear and uncertainty.

For years, Johnathon had been climbing the corporate ladder, working long hours and sacrificing his personal life in the pursuit of success. But despite all of his hard work, he had never felt truly fulfilled. He knew that he had more to offer the world than just making money for a faceless corporation.

And so, with a mixture of excitement and trepidation, Johnathon had decided to take a leap of faith and start his own business. He had spent months researching and planning, and he was confident that he had the knowledge and skills to make his venture a success.

But as he sat there in his new office, surrounded by empty desks and unfamiliar surroundings, Johnathon couldn't help but wonder if he had made the right decision. What if he had taken on too much risk? What if he failed?

As the hours ticked by, Johnathon threw himself into his work, determined to make the most of this new beginning. He poured over spreadsheets, made countless phone calls, and worked tirelessly to bring his vision to life.

Slowly but surely, things began to fall into place. Johnathon's business began to take shape, and he found himself surrounded by a team of passionate and talented individuals who shared his vision.

For the first time in years, Johnathon felt truly alive. He was no longer working for someone else's vision, but for his own. He was building something that would have a lasting impact on the world, and that thought filled him with a sense of purpose and drive that he had never experienced before.

As the weeks turned into months, Johnathon's business continued to thrive. He faced challenges and setbacks along the way, but he never lost sight of his vision or his determination to succeed.

And as he looked back on his decision to take a leap of faith and start his own business, Johnathon knew that it had been the best decision he had ever made. He was finally living a life of purpose and passion, and he knew that he would never go back to the soulless corporate world that he had left behind.

With a smile on his face and a sense of excitement in his heart, Johnathon knew that this was only the beginning of his journey. He was ready to face whatever challenges lay ahead, knowing that he had the courage and determination to overcome them.

A new beginning had indeed arrived, and Johnathon was ready to embrace it with open arms.

As the days went by, John found

himself growing more and more comfortable in his new role as the owner of his own business. He was working harder than he ever had before, but it was all worth it to see his dream coming to life.

One of the biggest challenges John faced in his new venture was finding the right employees. He knew that he couldn't do everything on his own, but he was also wary of trusting just anyone with his vision. It took months of searching, but eventually, John was able to assemble a team of dedicated and talented individuals who shared his passion for success.

With his team in place, John focused on growing his business. He worked tirelessly to build up his client base, and his efforts paid off as word of mouth spread about his company's exceptional service and quality work.

As the business began to thrive, John found himself facing new challenges. He had to learn how to manage his time effectively, balancing the demands of his work with his personal life. He also had to learn how to delegate tasks and trust his employees to handle important responsibilities.

But even as he faced these challenges, John felt more alive than he had in years. He was building something from scratch, something that was entirely his own. And as he watched his business grow and prosper, he knew that he had made the right decision in leaving his old job behind.

As he looked back on his journey, John realized that his new beginning had been the best thing that had ever happened to him. It had been a risk, to be sure, but it was a risk that had paid off in ways he had never imagined.

With a sense of pride and accomplishment, John knew that he had truly found his calling in life. And as he looked to the future, he was excited to see where his journey would take him next.

As the plane took off into the bright blue sky, Sarah felt a rush of excitement and nervousness. She was leaving behind everything she had ever known to start a new life in a new place. But she was also filled with a sense of hope and possibility, eager to see what opportunities and adventures lay ahead.

As the flight continued, Sarah's thoughts turned to the new beginning that awaited her. She had no idea what to expect, but she knew that she was ready for whatever came her way.

She had worked hard to get to this point, and she was determined to make the most of it.

As the plane began its descent, Sarah felt a flutter of anticipation in her stomach. She knew that this was just the beginning of her journey, and that there were sure to be many challenges and obstacles along the way. But she was ready for them. With a deep breath, she stepped off the plane and into a new chapter of her life.

Chapter Nine

Turning Points

As Johnathon continued to rise in the business world, he faced numerous challenges that tested his resolve and character. The most significant of these challenges came when he was tasked with leading a major company-wide restructuring that would require laying off a significant portion of the workforce.

At first, Johnathon saw this as just another necessary step in the pursuit of profits and growth. But as he began to see the faces of those who would be affected by the layoffs, he started to feel a sense of guilt and responsibility.

He struggled with this decision for weeks, losing sleep and becoming increasingly isolated from his friends and family. Eventually, he made the difficult choice to move forward with the restructuring, but he did so with a newfound commitment to treating those impacted with compassion and respect.

The experience was a turning point for Johnathon, causing him to question the value of profit at any cost and prompting him to reevaluate his priorities in life. He began to focus more on giving back to his community and investing in socially responsible initiatives, such as sustainable energy and education.

This shift in focus not only helped Johnathon feel more fulfilled in his personal life but also had a positive impact on his business ventures. By prioritizing social responsibility, Johnathon was able to attract and retain more employees who shared his values and build a reputation for his companies as ethical and responsible corporate citizens.

As Johnathon continued to pursue this new path, he faced new challenges and setbacks. But he also found new opportunities for growth and success, both in his personal life and in the business world.

Through it all, he remained committed to his core values of integrity, compassion, and social responsibility, recognizing that true wealth was about more than just money or power.

As Johnathon tried to wrap his head around the situation, he realized that he had to act fast. He couldn't let this opportunity slip away. He immediately got to work, putting together a team of lawyers and financial experts to help him navigate the complicated process of acquiring the company.

The next few weeks were a blur of meetings, negotiations, and legal documents. Johnathon worked tirelessly, hardly sleeping or eating, as he pushed to close the deal. His determination and drive impressed even his most seasoned colleagues, and he knew that this was the moment he had been waiting for.

Finally, after weeks of intense negotiations, Johnathon received the news he had been waiting for: the deal was done. He had successfully acquired the company, and he was now the proud owner of a major player in the industry.

The feeling of accomplishment was overwhelming, but Johnathon knew that this was only the beginning. With the acquisition under his belt, he had a newfound sense of confidence and a hunger for more. He had proven to himself and to the world that he was capable of achieving anything he set his mind to.

But as Johnathon sat in his new office, looking out at the city skyline, he couldn't help but feel a sense of emptiness. He had achieved so much, but at what cost? He had sacrificed his relationships, his health, and his values in the pursuit of success.

As he sat there, deep in thought, Johnathon realized that he needed to find a new path. He needed to redefine what success meant to him and find a way to balance his ambition with his personal life. It was a daunting task, but Johnathon knew that he was up to the challenge. He was ready for a new beginning.

The realization hit Johnathon like a ton of bricks. He had been so focused on his own goals and aspirations that he had neglected the people who truly mattered to him. He had pushed away his family, hurt his friends, and even compromised his own values. For the first time in a long time, Johnathon felt a deep sense of shame.

As he walked the deserted streets of the city, Johnathon began to reflect on his life and the choices he had made. He realized that he had been so consumed with his own ambition that he had lost sight of what was truly important in life. He thought of his parents, who had always supported him but whom he had ignored in his pursuit of success. He thought of his friends, who had been there for him through thick and thin, but whom he had abandoned in his pursuit of wealth. And he thought of himself, and the person he had become - someone who would do anything to get ahead, even if it meant sacrificing his own integrity.

As Johnathon walked, his thoughts turned to the future. He knew that he needed to make some changes in his life, to re-prioritize and to start living for something other than his own selfish desires. It wasn't going to be easy, but he was determined to make a fresh start.

With a new sense of purpose, Johnathon headed back to his apartment, ready to begin the next chapter of his life.

Chapter Ten

The Final Struggle

Johnathon sat alone in his office, surrounded by the trappings of his success. The walls were lined with framed photos of himself shaking hands with powerful politicians and business leaders. The shelves were filled with trophies and awards he had received over the years. But for the first time in his life, these things brought him no joy.

He couldn't shake the feeling that he had lost something important along the way. His relationships with his family and friends had suffered, and he had become so consumed with work that he barely had time for anything else. He knew that he had made sacrifices to get to where he was, but now he wondered if it had all been worth it.

As he sat there, lost in thought, his phone rang. It was his attorney, calling to inform him that the SEC was launching an investigation into his business practices. Johnathon's heart sank. He knew that this could mean the end of everything he had worked for.

He spent the next few days frantically trying to cover his tracks, but it was no use. The investigation was thorough, and soon the media got wind of what was happening. Johnathon's carefully constructed empire began to crumble before his eyes.

In the end, he was forced to sell off his assets and resign from his company. He was left with nothing but a tarnished reputation and the realization that he had lost sight of what was truly important in life.

But even as he faced the consequences of his actions, Johnathon knew that he had learned some valuable lessons. He realized that wealth and success were not the most important things in life, and that true happiness could not be bought with money. He also knew that he had to make amends for the harm he had caused to others.

With a newfound sense of purpose, Johnathon set out to make things right. He reconnected with his family and friends, and even began volunteering at a local charity. He knew that he could never undo the mistakes of his past, but he was determined to use his experiences to create a better future.

As he looked out at the city skyline, Johnathon felt a sense of peace that he had not experienced in years. He knew that he had finally found what he had been searching for all along - a new beginning.

He smiled as he thought about the journey he had been on, with all of its twists and turns. He had started out as a young and ambitious man, eager to prove himself in the world of business. But along the way, he had lost sight of what truly mattered.

Now, he was a different person - wiser, more compassionate, and more aware of the impact of his actions. He knew that he would never forget the lessons he had learned, and that they would guide him in everything he did from this point forward.

As he left his office for the last time,

Johnathon felt a sense of closure. He had come full circle, from the ambitious young man he had once been, to the humbled and introspective person he was now. He knew that his life would never be the same again, but he was ready for whatever lay ahead.

As he walked out into the bright sunshine, he felt a renewed sense of hope. The world was full of possibilities, and he was excited to explore them. For the first time in a long time, he felt truly alive.

As the final day of the trial approached, Johnathon felt a mix of emotions. He was anxious about the outcome, but also relieved that the end was near. He knew that he had done everything he could to defend himself, but there was always the possibility of an unfavorable verdict.

On the day of the trial, Johnathon arrived early to the courthouse, dressed in his best suit and tie. He felt a sense of gravity and importance as he walked into the courtroom, taking his seat at the defendant's table. The judge and jury were already present, and the room was buzzing with anticipation.

The trial was long and grueling, with both sides presenting their arguments and evidence. Johnathon's lawyers were skilled and experienced, but the prosecution was relentless in their pursuit of justice. The tension in the room was palpable as the jury was sent to deliberate.

Hours passed as Johnathon sat in the courtroom, waiting for a verdict. He felt his heart racing and his palms sweating with each passing moment. Finally, the jury returned with their decision.

The judge read the verdict aloud, and Johnathon could feel his heart sinking. He had been found guilty on all charges. His mind raced as he tried to process what this would mean for his future.

As he was escorted out of the courtroom in handcuffs, Johnathon knew that this was the end of the road for him. He had lost everything he had worked so hard to build, and now faced the prospect of spending years behind bars.

But as he looked back on his life and the choices he had made, Johnathon realized that he had been blinded by his own ambition. He had lost sight of what was truly important in life, and had paid the ultimate price for it.

In the end, Johnathon's story serves

as a cautionary tale about the dangers of unchecked ambition and the importance of staying true to one's values. As he walked away from the courthouse, he knew that he had a long road ahead of him, but he was determined to start anew and rebuild his life with a newfound sense of purpose and humility. The final struggle had been won, but at a cost that Johnathon would never forget.

Conclusion

Wealth is a story about one man's pursuit of success and the toll it takes on him and those around him. Johnathon Richards started out as a young and ambitious employee, determined to make a name for himself in the business world. Through his relentless drive and unwavering determination, he rose to the top, becoming a wealthy and powerful businessman.

But as Johnathon's wealth and power grew, he became increasingly isolated from those around him. His family, friends, and even his own sense of morality took a backseat to his pursuit of success. He made deals and took risks that ultimately led him down a dangerous path, where he was forced to confront the consequences of his actions.

Throughout his journey, Johnathon faced numerous ethical dilemmas that challenged him and forced him to question everything he had worked for. But in the end, he emerged stronger, wiser, and humbled by the experiences that had shaped him.

The story of Wealth serves as a cautionary tale about the dangers of greed and the importance of staying true to one's values. It shows that success is not just about accumulating wealth and power, but also about maintaining meaningful relationships and staying grounded in one's principles.

As the final chapter comes to a close, Johnathon realizes that the true wealth in his life was not his monetary assets, but the relationships he had built and the lessons he had learned. The journey may have been tumultuous, but in the end, it was all worth it.

www.ingramcontent.com/pod-product-compliance
Lightning Source LLC
Chambersburg PA
CBHW070920220526
45467CB00004B/1483